Miami

Miami

A Downtown America Book

Marsha Fischer

dP Dillon Press, Inc. Minneapolis, MN 55415

Photographic Acknowledgments

Photos have been reproduced through the courtesy of James Blank; Brian Parker/Tom Stack Photos; Walter Marks/Metro Dade County; Cameramann International; the Historical Association of Southern Florida; the Port of Miami; Greater Miami Convention and Visitors Bureau; the Miami Metrozoo; and Biscayne National Park. Cover photo by James Blank.

Library of Congress Cataloging-in-Publication Data

Fischer, Marsha.
  Miami / Marsha Fischer.
    p. cm. — (A Downtown America book)
    Summary: Explores the city of Miami, both past and present, describing neighborhoods, attractions, festivals, and historic sites.
  ISBN 0-87518-428-6 (lib. bdg): $12.95
  1. Miami (Fla.)—Juvenile literature. [1. Miami (Fla.)]
I. Title. II. Series.
F319.M6F57 1990
975.9'381—dc20
                            89-25694
                               CIP
                               AC

Dillon Press, Inc., 242 Portland Avenue South
Minneapolis, Minnesota 55415

Printed in the United States of America
1 2 3 4 5 6 7 8 9 10 99 98 97 96 95 94 93 92 91 90

About the Author

As a resident of South Florida, Marsha Fischer finds Miami one of the more exciting and beautiful cities in the area. She has had opportunity to research and write about Miami as an analyst for a local real estate firm, and as a freelance writer. Ms. Fischer currently lives in Plantation, Florida, with her husband and child.

Contents

City Seal.

Fast Facts about Miami

Miami: City of Tomorrow; the Magic City

Location: Southeastern tip of the Florida Peninsula; Biscayne Bay and the Atlantic Ocean lie to the east and south, the Everglades to the west, and Broward County to the north

Area: City, 54 square miles (140 square kilometers), including 20 square miles (52 square kilometers) of inland water; consolidated metropolitan area, 2,000 square miles (5,200 square kilometers)

Population (1988 estimate*): City, 342,315; consolidated metropolitan area, 1.8 million

Major Population Groups: Whites, Hispanics, Blacks

Altitude: Highest—10 feet (27 meters); lowest—sea level

Climate: Average temperature is 69°F (21°C) in January, 82°F (33°C) in July; average annual precipitation is 59 inches (5 centimeters)

Founding Date: 1896

City Seal: A palm tree stands in the center of the seal, surrounded by "The City of Miami" on top, and "Dade Co., Florida" at the bottom, all of which is surrounded by a circular gold braid

City Flag: The city of Miami does not have an official city flag

Form of Government: Commission-manager; a mayor is elected to a two-year term, and four commissioners to four-year terms; the commission appoints a city manager; Miami is also run by a metropolitan county government called *MetroDade*; the nine-member Dade County Board of Commissioners heads MetroDade

Important Industries: Tourism, banking, building supplies, retail

*Official 1990 U.S. Bureau of the Census figures available in 1991-92.

Festivals and Parades

January: Miccosukee Indian Arts Festival; Art Deco Weekend; Key Biscayne Art Festival

February: Scottish Festival and Games; Miami Film Festival; Coconut Grove Art Festival

March: Carnival Miami; Calle Ocho

April: Bounty of the Sea Seafood Festival; Miami Magic; River Cities Festival (focuses on the Miami River and its environment)

May: Hispanic Theater Festival

June: Goombay Festival (celebrates Bahamian and African-American culture)

September: Festival Miami

October: Oktoberfest; Hispanic Heritage Festival; West Indian American Miami Carnival

November: Cornucopia of the Arts; Banyan Art Festival

December: Sunstreet Festival; Holiday Boat Parade; Art in the Heart of Miami Beach; Orange Bowl Jamboree; Junior Orange Bowl Festival; King Mango Strut

For further information about festivals and parades, see the agencies listed on page 57.

United States

Miami

FLORIDA

Miami

N

MIAMI CANAL

OVERTOWN

Morningside
Park

LITTLE
HAITI

JULIA TUTTLE CAUSEWAY

MIAMI BEACH

MIAMI

Watson
Park

MIAMI RIVER

Bayfront
Park

① ② ③

PORT
OF MIAMI

FLAGLER STREET

CALLE OCHO

LITTLE
HAVANA

RICKENBACKER

④ ⑤ CAUSEWAY

VIRGINIA
KEY

CORAL
GABLES

⑥

⑧

⑦

Crandon
County
Park

NORTH
ATLANTIC
OCEAN

COCONUT
GROVE

Points of Interest

① Civic Center
② Orange Bowl
③ MetroDade Cultural Center
④ Museum of Science
⑤ Villa Vizcaya
⑥ Seaquarium
⑦ Planet Ocean
⑧ University of Miami
⑨ Fairchild Tropical Garden
⑩ Parrot Jungle
⑪ Metrozoo

KEY
BISCAYNE

BISCAYNE BAY

GULF STREAM

⑨

Cape Florida
State Park

⑪ ⑩

miles 0 2 4
kilometers 0 2 4

1

Welcome to Miami

When you picture Miami, do you see tall, gleaming skyscrapers or soft, sandy beaches? Maybe you think of a place where Spanish is spoken more often than English. Perhaps you imagine a city where more retired people live than working people or schoolchildren. Which Miami is the real Miami? The answer is all of these.

Through the window of an airplane flying into Miami, only the pine forests of the Everglades can be seen. Suddenly, the city appears beyond the trees and seagrass. As the plane gets ready to land, it flies above the Atlantic Ocean before turning toward the Miami Airport. Passengers can glimpse the rows of hotels along the shores of Miami Beach.

Miami is the southernmost city in the mainland United States. Located at the tip of Florida, it is bor-

Rows of hotels line the shore of Miami Beach.

dered by the Atlantic Ocean, Biscayne Bay, and the Everglades. Whenever there is a day off from work or school, many Miamians head for one of 16 public beaches in the area for a day of swimming and sailing.

Some of these beaches are across Biscayne Bay from downtown Miami, on a narrow strip of land that was once a sandbar surrounded by swamps. This island is Miami Beach, a separate city from Miami. In the bay between Miami and Miami Beach lie several small islands. Some of these islands have huge homes on them, while others are unused—except by wildlife. Six island-hopping causeways, or bridges, connect Miami Beach to Miami.

Downtown Miami is a mix of wide boulevards, narrow streets, and lively activity. Cars, trucks, and buses fill the streets. To help with traffic problems, there is the PeopleMover. This mini-monorail track carries passengers around the central part of the city.

The people of Miami come from almost every city in the United States and nearly every country in the world. Some are attracted by the warm weather, cool ocean breezes, and the hope of freedom and opportunity. Others came to Miami because they thought they could improve their standard of living in the United States. Today, nearly 40 percent of Miamians are Hispanic, while 15 percent are black.

The Lummus Park beach is a favorite spot for both tourists and Miamians.

For almost 100 years, Miamians have worked to clear the thick mangrove swamps and pine forests that once stood where the city is today. Tall sawgrass has been replaced with condominiums and high-rise office buildings.

One well-known Miami skyscraper can be seen on reruns of the popular television series, "Miami Vice." Located on Brickell Avenue, the Aquitectonica Building has a 37-square foot (3.3-square meter) space between its tenth and fourteenth floors. A single palm tree sits in the middle of this space.

Most people consider the center of Miami to be the Omni. This black, 20-story tower contains a hotel and shopping mall. It combines two of Miami's biggest industries—tourism and shopping—under one roof.

Miami has many skyscrapers, but it has not always been easy to build them. Much of the city is built on sand and swamps. In fact, most of Miami is only 6 feet (1.8 meters) above sea level. Construction crews solve this problem by stacking piles of soil on the ground to build up the level of the land.

The holes left by the bulldozers fill with water and become lakes and canals. Children, too, can form their own "pools" in their backyards. Water is so close to the surface that even shallow holes become filled with water. This is why Miami homes do not have basements.

Besides being very close to sea

The Aquitectonica Building is a Miami landmark.

level, Miami is also very flat. There is only one natural hill in the city. It was formed more than 100,000 years ago, when Miami was covered by a shallow sea. Fast currents rolled up little balls of limestone, creating a two-mile (three-kilometer)-long ridge scientists call the Miami Oolite. Main Highway in Coconut Grove, a neighborhood of Miami, follows the path of the ridge.

Miami is closer to the equator than any other city in the mainland United States. Because of its location,

it has only two seasons. The rainy season lasts from May to October, and the dry season runs from November to April. More rain can fall in one day during the rainy season than in the entire dry season.

During the rainy season, hurricanes sometimes strike Miami. Hurricanes have played an important part in the city's history. Miami suffered heavy damage from these storms twice, once in 1926 and again in 1935. Hundreds of people lost their lives, and many buildings were destroyed. Government officials hope to avoid such losses if a hurricane should hit modern Miami. New buildings are designed to stand against hurricane-force winds, and residents have safety drills each year.

The same wet, hot air and unstable atmosphere that create hurricanes also produce lightning. The state of Florida is the unofficial lightning capital of the country—lightning hits Miami an average of 76 days each year.

Summers in Miami are long, hot, and humid. Ocean breezes help to keep the city cooler than some northern inland Florida cities. Still, on most summer days, Miamians try to stay inside their air-conditioned homes, cars, and offices.

Winters in Miami are mild. Local residents think that temperatures near 50°F (10°C) are cold, because the average temperature for January is 66°F (10°C)! During the winter of 1977, though, Miamians were sur-

Modern buildings in downtown Miami are built to be hurricane-proof.

prised by snow flurries that lasted for a whole day. Children were let out of school and people left work early to touch the snow. Even though less than an inch stayed on the ground, Miami residents still talk about it.

The weather has always been an important force in Miami. It draws the tourists the city's economy depends on. It also helps create the natural beauty Miamians are so proud of. In fact, if it did not have such mild winters, Miami might not exist today.

2

Miami Past and Present

The first European to see southern Florida was a shipwrecked Spanish sailor in the late 1400s. For a long time after that, only the Tequesta Indians lived in the soggy marshes in the south.

As settlers from the northeastern United States moved into northern and central Florida in the early 1800s, the Tequesta Indians were forced off their lands and into the Everglades.

They began raiding some settlements, trying to regain their land. To protect the settlers, the United States government built forts in Florida. In 1836, during the Second Seminole War, Fort Dallas was built where the Miami River meets Biscayne Bay.

In the late 1880s, the area north of modern Miami started changing. The cattle and farming communities there became resort areas. Wealthy

The Everglades are now a part of a national park.

Julia Tuttle.

people came to the hotels to get away from cold winters in the North. The sounds of sledgehammers filled the air as Henry Flagler began building the Florida East Coast Railroad down the coast of Florida.

Julia Tuttle from Cleveland, a winter resident of Miami, tried for several years to convince Flagler to bring the railroad to Miami. Flagler, though, saw no reason to build the railroad past Palm Beach, about 100 miles (161 kilometers) north of the Miami area.

Then in 1894, a frost hit Florida. It killed citrus trees and other plants as far south as Palm Beach. Yet orange blossoms still bloomed in Miami.

A stubborn woman, Tuttle sent Flagler a sprig of orange blossoms and

Circus elephants were used to clear the swampland on Miami Beach.

green leaves. She sent another invitation to come to Miami, too. This time, Flagler came. He agreed to build the railroad line to Miami, and the city's first boom began. Between 1896 and 1900, the population grew from 800 to more than 1,600.

Wars helped the young city continue to grow. Since Miami was only 90 miles (145 kilometers) away from Cuba, a training center for the soldiers fighting in the Spanish-American War was set up there in 1898. Many soldiers stayed in Miami after the war.

Then in 1913, John Collins and Carl Fisher, two Miami residents, built a bridge across Biscayne Bay. This connected Miami Beach to the mainland. Circus elephants helped clear the land, and soon resort hotels replaced swamps.

Later that year, though, Henry Flagler died. Flagler had provided much of the money used to improve the city. Without his support, a number of businesses closed, and many people lost their jobs.

John Deering helped save the city. His family had been wintering in the Miami area for several years. Deering decided he and his family should have a winter home of their own. His plans for a small house grew into a copy of an Italian villa. Villa Vizcaya, as it is called, is complete with formal gardens and two mazes.

The clattering of bicycles filled the air as thousands of people rushed to work on the mansion. Today, Vizcaya is a museum. Many visitors take the guided tour of the mansion's rooms and gardens.

During World War I, Miami was a training center for pilots. Not only rich tourists, but daring young men were now coming to Miami. Many of the soldiers that were stationed in the city returned with their families after the war.

In the early 1920s, Miami was one of the most popular cities in the United States. Gangster Al Capone and many movie stars had homes in Miami. So did some of America's

The Villa Vizcaya house and gardens.

wealthiest families. During this time, the whole state of Florida was changing. The Everglades were being drained, and people bought the land as soon as it was for sale.

The city grew in size very quickly. People said Miami would stretch from the Atlantic Ocean to the Gulf of Mexico, on the western edge of the state, and that the Everglades would disappear entirely. So many canals were cut while draining the Everglades that bridges and causeways had to be built to link the city together. By the end of the 1920s, Miami was Florida's second largest city.

But much of Miami was destroyed by the hurricane of 1926, which killed nearly 400 people. Nine years later, another hurricane washed out the railroad tracks that connected the Florida Keys to Miami. When local businesses failed, many residents moved north in search of work.

Once again, a war brought Miami back to life. During World War II, the area was a naval and aviation training center. After the war, soldiers returned for vacations with their families. Miami's tourist industry grew.

During the 1940s and 1950s, with the invention of air conditioning, people moved to Miami in large numbers. By 1960, only one of every four people living in Miami had been born there.

Miami changed from a sleepy little town into an international city in the 1960s when people from Latin America arrived by the thousands.

This photo shows some of the damage caused by the 1926 Miami hurricane.

Many immigrants from Cuba came to Miami after Fidel Castro took power in that country in 1959.

In the 1970s and early 1980s, another wave of immigrants came to Miami. Many of these were from Haiti, an island in the Caribbean Sea.

They left the island because of political and economic problems. Then, during the spring of 1980, Fidel Castro suddenly let more than 130,000 Cubans leave that country. Most of them had been in Cuban jails. Fishing boats, sailboats, and pleasure boats crowded Miami's coast. These new Cubans were not easily accepted by Miamians. It was hard to separate the real criminals from those who had been arrested for disagreeing with the Cuban government.

Miami has faced many problems over the years. The drug trade was a major concern in the late 1970s and 1980s. At this time, Miami was the arrival point for most of the marijuana and cocaine coming into the United States. Then, the Coast Guard increased its patrols. Tougher laws were passed, too, which make it easier to send drug dealers to jail. While it is harder to smuggle drugs into Miami than it once was, drug abuse and drug-related crimes are still a problem in the city.

Construction and new growth are also a concern to Miamians. Some residents are worried that the city might outgrow its resources, especially its drinking water.

Miami gets its drinking water from the Biscayne Aquifer, an underground reservoir. Only a thin layer of limestone separates the fresh water from the ocean salt water. Whenever there is a drought, limits are put on water usage. If a drought lasts too long, the barrier between the salt and the fresh water can break down. The salt water would then become mixed with the drinking water, making it unsafe to drink. The bigger Miami's population becomes, the more water is needed. Some people want to stop turning the Everglades into homes,

shopping centers, and businesses in order to protect the water supply from further damage.

Many residents are also worried about the environment. The land along the beaches is being worn away by waves, rain, and wind. Millions of dollars were spent to rebuild ten miles of Miami Beach, but more money will have to be spent to fight nature and prevent the beach from wearing away completely.

Hotels and condominiums have been built right to the ocean's edge. If a beach is washed into the sea, the buildings could be destroyed. Also, without the beach to act as a buffer,

millions of dollars worth of property could be damaged, and lives could be lost when the next hurricane hits Miami.

Despite their problems, Miami and Miamians continue to look to the future. From the time that Julia Tuttle showed Henry Flagler that the sun shined bright in Miami, people have been coming to the city. Some come to escape cold weather for a while, some come in search of political freedom, and some come just to enjoy the beach and the sun. All of these different people make Miami an exciting, world-class city.

MIAMI PEPES
FERRETERIA
ENTRADA PRINCIPAL
HERRAMIENTAS,
MIAMI PEPES"
FERRETERIA
IMPORTAMOS Y
EXPORTAMOS
MATERIALES
DE
CONSTRUCCION
MADERAS
PLYWOOD Y
ACE
HARDWARE
ARTICULOS
PARA EL
HOGAR
Regalos
PULL
MIAMI
PEPE'S
FERRETERIA
HARDWARE
ENTRADA

3

An International City

Walk down almost any street in Miami, and you will hear languages from around the world. In Little Haiti, you might hear French, or a combination of French and English. In Little Havana, Spanish is spoken by many residents. Both these neighborhoods were formed by immigrants who wanted to live and work near people from their homelands. Other neighborhoods were created by busi-nesspeople in the 1920s to sell real estate. Here, you might hear Italian, English, Swedish, or German spoken by visitors or Miamians. No matter why they were formed, Miami's neighborhoods give the city its lively look and spirit.

Many of Miami's neighborhoods began as individual cities created at the beginning of the twentieth century. As the cities grew, they spread

A hardware store in Little Havana.

closer to the city of Miami. Some of them became part of the city, while others remained separate. When Miami started changing from a small tourist town to a modern city in the early 1960s, each city had its own police, fire, and sanitation departments. This created some problems, and local politicians realized they would have to cooperate in order to grow.

Eventually, the city of Miami and its nearest neighbors created the nation's first metropolitan government. They called it MetroDade, because Miami and its surrounding cities are all in Dade County.

Community leaders next looked for ways to join the different cities together. They created Metrorail, a

monorail linking downtown Miami to southern suburbs. The first part of this system opened in 1985. In time, it will connect all parts of the city and metropolitan area to downtown.

One of the cities that was helped by both MetroDade and Metrorail was Coral Gables. It is an independent city surrounded on all sides by Miami. George Merrick designed and planned Coral Gables so that people could live, work, and shop there. Even though he was only able to finish part of the city, his plan still controls the arrangement of the streets and the design of the homes. The University of Miami, home of the nationally-ranked Hurricane football team, is in Coral Gables.

Northeast of Coral Gables lies

Metrorail's lighted tracks help carry commuters into downtown Miami.

Coconut Grove, the oldest part of Miami. Most of the streets here are paved with bricks and lined with lights that look like old-fashioned gas lamps. Some of the oldest buildings in southern Florida still stand in the neighborhood. Plymouth Congregational Church, built in 1897, is the first church built in the area. Just around the corner is the city's first school house.

Coconut Grove has become an important center for arts and entertainment. People sip coffee at the sidewalk cafes that line Main Highway, the main street in Coconut Grove. Art collectors visit the many galleries for which the Grove is famous, and tourists walk along the streets.

A few miles to the east of Coconut Grove, across Biscayne Bay, is Miami Beach. The Art Deco District on Miami Beach was developed in the 1930s. Most of the buildings here are in the Art Deco or Spanish Mediterranean Revival style. They are painted in light colors—shades of pink, white, peach, and aqua. This building style also features rounded corners and windows that are designed to catch the cool breezes.

By the 1970s, many of these buildings had begun to fall apart. When the Art Deco District was declared a national historical area in 1979, the buildings were saved from the wrecking ball. Today, many young professionals have moved into the area and are repairing the buildings.

The Art Deco District is one of

Buildings in the Art Deco District.

the most popular places to live in the Miami area. It is also one of the most active. Each January, a section of the beach is closed off for the Art Deco Festival. Jazz bands play music from the 1920s and 1930s, and some residents wear clothing from that era.

To the northwest of downtown Miami is Overtown. It was created for black residents in 1896 when Miami was a segregated city. At that time, Miami had laws which forced blacks and whites to live apart from each other. Segregation was outlawed in the 1960s, and blacks and whites were allowed to live wherever they chose. Many black residents chose to stay in Overtown, where their families, friends, and businesses were.

In the 1940s and 1950s, Overtown was a lively, active neighborhood. Well-known entertainers, such as Louis Armstrong and Lena Horne, performed in the area's many jazz clubs. But Overtown was nearly destroyed in the 1960s when two big expressways were built through the center of the neighborhood. Because of this, many businesses and some people left the area.

Overtown was in a state of neglect in 1980. After five white policemen were found innocent of beating and killing a black insurance salesman, riots broke out. Many residents felt that the riots were the only way to show their anger at what they thought was a bad decision by the jury.

At that time, a group was formed to find ways to encourage businesses to move back to Overtown. They hoped this would help bring new life to the area. In 1989, however, more riots followed a police shooting of two black men. Once again, community leaders met to find ways to solve the area's problems. As new businesses open and more jobs are created, some Overtown residents hope to become an important part of Miami once more.

On the opposite side of the city, between downtown Miami and Coral Gables, lies an area called Little

Joe Robbie Stadium, in the Overtown neighborhood, was home to the 1989 Super Bowl.

Havana. Almost everyone in Little Havana speaks Spanish. Many do not speak English at all. In fact, Little Havana's main street is called *Calle Ocho*, which means Eighth Street in Spanish.

Every February, the neighborhood comes alive when Cuban culture is celebrated with the Calle Ocho Festival. Dancers in colorful costumes perform traditional Cuban dances, and the street music has a Latin beat to it.

Cubans affect the city's economy

Hispanic Miamians take part in the Calle Ocho Festival.

and politics. In 1985, Xavier Suarez, a Cuban-born American, was elected mayor of Miami. Cubans also affect the music in Miami. Throughout the 1980s, Gloria Estefan, a Cuban American, and the Miami Sound Machine could be heard on radios across the United States. They play a mix of American rock-and-roll, Cuban folk music, and Caribbean music.

Just as Little Havana reminds many people of Cuba, Little Haiti looks similar to Port-au-Prince, the capital of Haiti. People here speak a language which is a mixture of their native language—French—and English.

In Little Haiti, shops sell goods which appeal to Haitians, such as *griat* (fried lamb) and *passot* (fried goat).

The different ethnic groups in Miami do not always understand and cooperate with each other. Many residents believe the large number of immigrants make jobs hard to find. At times, these racial tensions lead to violence, such as the January 1989 riots.

Overtown residents say the cause of the conflicts is the lack of opportunity African Americans have had in Miami. Hispanics and blacks in Miami compete for government aid and jobs. There is not enough money to give housing and job training to everyone who needs it. In 1988 and 1989, unemployment among Miami's black residents rose to 10 percent. Unemployment among Cubans, however, fell to below 6 percent.

Local groups and community leaders work hard to help all Miamians understand and appreciate their different ways of life.

A community project called "World of Difference" shows people the good that each ethnic group has brought to the city. As a part of this program, teachers go to special classes. When they return to their schools, they share what they have learned with students and other teachers. Community leaders want the people of Miami to learn about the traditions and history of all of their neighbors. In this way, they hope Miamians will learn to respect each other and enjoy the beautiful city they have created.

4

Miami at Work

Many of Miami's industries can be traced back to the city's early days. Shopping, shipping, and tourism are especially important. They have added to the Miami way of life.

William and Mary Brickell were among Miami's first shopkeepers. Today, thousands of people work in the retail business. Burdines, a Miami-based department store, is one of the city's biggest employers.

People from all over South Florida and South America come to Miami to shop. Some of the best bargains can be found at the discount shops in the Fashion District. Expensive clothing can be sold at low prices because Miami is one of the largest clothing producers in the United States. Shoes, shorts, and children's clothing are all made here.

Another big business centers

Cruise ships and freighters dock at the Port of Miami.

Vacationers wave from the deck of a large cruise ship.

around the Port of Miami, the busiest cruise port in the world. Ships line up one after another at the pier, like cars parked along the curb. More than 2 million people each year take cruises to the Caribbean, South America, and other places on ships that sail out of Miami. Carnival Cruise Line, one of the world's largest cruise lines, has its home offices here.

In addition to cruise ships, freighters and naval ships from all over the world dock in Miami. Tons of sugar, cement products, and frozen foods are among the goods shipped from the Port of Miami to Latin America, Europe, and Africa.

Ocean liners, oil tankers, and aircraft carriers also dock at the Port of Miami. Sailors from these vessels stroll through the streets, enjoying their holidays.

These international sailors are just one group among many that visit Miami every year. The tourist season starts in late November and ends in April. During these months, there is more traffic in the streets and longer lines at movies and restaurants. The change between tourist season and non-tourist season happens very quickly. Miamians say they don't need a calendar to know when Thanksgiving is!

The tourist industry has been through many changes. Originally, wealthy people from the northeastern United States came to spend winters in the warm sunshine. Then, in the 1950s and 1960s, Miami was a family vacation spot. Every winter, parents and children came to the city to enjoy the warm weather. When Walt Disney World opened in Orlando in the mid-1970s, though, many families stopped traveling as far as Miami.

In the late 1970s and 1980s, Central Americans and South Americans began visiting Miami. Some from lands south of the equator came to the area in the summer, when it was winter in their homelands. Others came simply to enjoy the beaches, the sun, and the shopping. The newcomers made Miami's tourist industry active year-round.

Businesspeople come to Miami, too. The city has become America's gateway to trade with Latin America because it is close to many Central and South American cities. The large number of Spanish-speaking people in the city makes it a good choice for companies doing business with Latin American firms. More than 100 international companies have their regional offices in Miami.

Miamians of Cuban heritage have been very important to business and industry in Miami. When Cubans started arriving in the city in the early 1960s, they often brought nothing with them but the desire to succeed. Many started businesses and gave jobs to those Cubans who came to Miami later. Within a few years, many of the immigrants were as well off as they had been when they left Cuba. Cuban Americans own several of Miami's biggest businesses, including one of the largest car dealerships in South Florida. Some have done especially well in banking.

Of the more than 70 banks in Miami, most can be found near the heart of Miami's financial district, Brickell Avenue. Brickell Avenue is sometimes called the "Wall Street of the South." Miami has more foreign banks than any other city in the country except New York City. The financial industry creates many jobs for computer programmers and operators.

To take care of its growing popu-

Brickell Avenue has been called the "Wall Street of the South."

lation, Miami has several hospitals and medical centers. Jackson Memorial Hospital and the University of Miami Medical School often cooperate on research projects. Together, they employ more than 10,000 people.

The manufacture of medical equipment for these and other medical centers nationwide also provides Miamians with many jobs. In 1959, Wallace Coulter invented the first instrument for counting blood cells. Today, the Miami-based Coulter Elec-

tronics Company makes machines for testing chocolates, paints, and cosmetics, as well as blood.

In addition to being a center for banking and medicine, Miami is also the home of many film studios. The city's scenery and weather make it a good place for filming such movies as *Flight of the Navigator* and *Making Mr. Right*. Also, the largest post-production studio outside of Los Angeles, California, opened here in 1985. This studio is responsible for editing movies once they have been filmed.

In 1980, Miami's leaders wanted to attract private industry to Liberty City and Overtown. These Miami neighborhoods had become run-down. Officials created "enterprise zones" in those areas. Businesses were given tax breaks on real estate to encourage them to open new offices. A variety of small manufacturers opened offices in Overtown. While these "enterprise zones" have not solved the area's problems, residents and officials alike hope they will create jobs and hope for the future.

Miami has grown from a little trading post to a seasonal resort town to a busy center for business and trade. Enterprises from each period remain, and new businesses continue to develop as Miami prepares for the next century.

A scene from *Flight of the Navigator*, which was filmed in Miami.

5

Sun, Surf, and Symphonies

Resting under a palm tree on a sandy beach, playing in the salty surf, or sailing in the warm waters of Biscayne Bay—these are just a few ways to have fun in Miami. Yet Miami has much more to offer.

In the past, people said that Miami was a city with no interest in music or the arts. Today, that situation has changed. Miami is the home of the New World Orchestra. Students from music schools such as Juilliard work hard to be selected for this symphony. Many of its musicians go on to play with well-known orchestras across the country.

Since 1985, Miami has also been the home of the Miami City Ballet. The ballet has become one of the most successful in the country. Miamians look forward to the dances the company creates each season.

Young Miamians create sand sculptures for one of the city's many festivals.

A "hands-on" iceberg exhibit at Planet Ocean.

While the city has much to offer to those interested in music, it also has many attractions for people interested in nature. The ocean is a strong force in Miami. In fact, there is a museum devoted to it and all of its wonders. At Planet Ocean, visitors can see the birth of the ocean, experience a hurricane, and touch an iceberg.

Across the street from Planet Ocean is the Miami Seaquarium, where the movie and television show "Flipper" was filmed. Here, visitors watch seals, sea lions, and Flipper's relatives, the dolphins, perform.

Metrozoo, in southwest Miami, is a different kind of zoo. There are no cages. Only deep moats separate the animals from the visitors. Metrozoo's

Show time at the Miami Seaquarium.

This hornbill is one of 70 species of birds at Miami Metrozoo.

breeding program is very successful, and many baby animals are born each year. This helps several endangered species, such as the white Bengal tiger and the Indian rhinoceros, to survive. The zoo is also home to more than 70 species of birds, which soar above visitors' heads inside a special large net.

The birds fly completely free at Parrot Jungle. Most of the birds do not stray, but once in a while a nearby resident will be surprised to see a brightly plumed bird in her yard.

Besides animals, Miami has many unusual plants. The largest tropical botanical garden in the United States is Fairchild Tropical Gardens in Coral Gables. While wandering winding paths through a rain forest, palm glade, or sunken garden, visitors can discover hundreds of kinds of palms, orchids, and other tropical plants.

For those interested in sports, Miami hosts activities throughout the year. One of Miami's important annual events is the Orange Bowl football game. Two of the best major college football teams are selected to play in this New Year's Day event.

Foot races, tennis games, and parades fill the week before the big game. Children's groups from all over Florida make floats for the Junior Orange Bowl Parade. The float that wins is able to take part in the King Orange Jamboree Parade on New Year's Eve.

Sports fans can find a team to cheer for year-round. Miami is the home of the Dolphins, the first National Football League team to remain unbeaten for an entire season. The Super Bowl has been played in Miami five times. The last time was at the new Joe Robbie Stadium in northwest Miami in 1989.

Professional basketball has come to Miami, too. The Miami Heat had the worst start of any team in the NBA, losing 17 games before finally winning one. Faithful fans continue to come to watch the team play, though, hoping for more victories.

Each spring, Miami is the home of baseball's Baltimore Orioles. After spring training, the major league team returns to Baltimore. The players who are not chosen to play for the Orioles remain in Miami, playing in the "Grapefruit League."

This large sea fan and elk horn coral are part of the coral reef in Biscayne National Park.

Greater Miami is covered with parks, including two national parks, two state parks, and dozens of county and city parks. The Everglades National Park is the most famous in the area. Visitors can canoe and hike through more than 1 million acres (400,000 hectares) of forest, swampland, and marshy areas. They might catch a glimpse of alligators, rare birds, and other wildlife.

In recent years, the plants and wildlife in the park have been threatened by nearby construction and pollution. People who want to preserve Florida's natural heritage are fighting to protect the park's plant and animal life.

Biscayne National Park, one of the nation's newest parks, lies just south of downtown Miami. All but a small part of the park is under water. It features part of the only living coral reef in the United States. Visitors enjoy snorkeling, scuba diving, and sailing here.

Tamiami Park, in the western part of the city, was once an airport. Now it is home for the largest youth baseball league in the country, the largest solar-heated pool, and every March, the largest youth fair.

Miami is no longer the swampy, lonely outpost it was 100 years ago. Nor is it just a place to have fun in the sun. As a modern, international city, today's Miami offers a wide variety of things to do for people of many different cultures and life-styles. Miamians hope their city's many strengths and attractions will keep it thriving for the next 100 years and beyond.

Places to Visit in Miami

Art Museums

Bacardi Art Gallery
2100 Biscayne Boulevard
(305) 573-8511

Bass Museum
212 Park Avenue
(305) 673-7533

Center for the Fine Arts
101 W. Flagler Street
(305) 375-1700

Cuban Museum of Art and Culture
1300 S.W. 12th Avenue
(305) 858-8006

Metropolitan Museum and Art Center
1212 Anastasia Avenue
(305) 442-1448

Science Museums

Museum of Science
4280 S. Miami Avenue
(305) 854-4247

Planet Ocean
Rickenbacker Causeway
(305) 361-9455

Weeks Air Museum
14710 S. W. 128th Street
(305) 235-5197

Historical Museums

Barnacle State Historic Site
3485 Main Highway
(305) 448-9445

Gold Coast Railroad Museum
12450 S. W. 152nd Street
(305) 253-0063

Historical Museum of South Florida
Dade Cultural Center
101 W. Flagler Street
(305) 375-1492

Villa Vizcaya
3251 S. Miami Avenue
(305) 579-2813

Performing Arts

Coconut Grove Playhouse
3500 Main Highway
(305) 442-4000

Gusman Center
174 E. Flagler Street
(305) 372-0925

Miami Arena
721 N.W. First Avenue
(305) 374-6877

Miami City Ballet
905 Lincoln Road
(305) 532-4880

Other Attractions

Coral Castle
28655 S. Dixie Highway
(305) 248-6344

Fairchild Tropical Garden
10901 Old Clutler Road
(305) 667-1651

Metrozoo
12400 S.W. 152nd Street
(305) 251-0400

Miami Seaquarium
4400 Rickenbacker Causeway
(305) 361-5703

Monkey Jungle
14805 S.W. 216th Street
(305) 235-1611

Parrot Jungle and Gardens
11000 S.W. 57th Avenue
(305) 666-7834

Additional information can be obtained from these agencies:

Greater Miami Convention and Visitors Bureau
701 Brickell Avenue
Miami, FL 33131
(305) 350-7700

Greater Miami Chamber of Commerce
Omni International
1601 Biscayne Boulevard
Miami, FL 33131
(305) 573-4300

Miami: A Historical Time Line

1836   Fort Dallas is founded

1875   Julia Tuttle comes to Miami

1896   Henry Flagler extends the Florida East Coast Railroad to Miami; the City of Miami is incorporated

1898   The Spanish-American War begins; troops train in Miami

1912   Overseas Railroad is opened

1913   Henry Flagler dies

1914   Construction on Villa Vizcaya begins; a bridge connecting Miami Beach to the mainland opens

1920   The Everglades drainage project begins, creating start of Florida land boom

1926   A hurricane hits Miami, destroying property and killing hundreds

1931   Airline service is established between Miami and New York City

1933   The first Orange Bowl game takes place

1960   Mass Cuban immigration begins

1970s   Haitian immigrants come to Miami

1977   Snow falls in Miami for the first time in recorded history

1980   Riots start after white police are found not guilty in the murder of a black insurance salesman; the Mariel boatlift brings thousands of Cuban immigrants to Miami

1985   Metrorail begins operating

1987   Joe Robbie Stadium opens

1989   Riots start when an off-duty policeman shoots two blacks; the first Super Bowl to be held in Miami in 10 years is played at the new Joe Robbie Stadium

Index